The Great RhiNo ReScue

Saving the
Southern
White Rhinos

Sandra Markle

Millbrook Press • Minneapolis

For Linda Wolfe and the students of Seven Hills School in Cincinnati, Ohio

Acknowledgments: The author would like to thank the following people for sharing their enthusiasm and expertise: Dr. William Fowlds, wildlife veterinarian, the Wilderness Foundation Medivet Project Coordinator; Dr. Lorinda Hern, Cofounder of the Rhino Rescue Project; Henry Holsthyzen, K9 Security Solutions; and Dr. Richard Vigne, Chief Executive Officer at Ol Pejeta Conservancy. A special thank-you to Skip Jeffery for his loving support during the creative process.

Millbrook Press
A division of Lerner Publishing Group, Inc.
241 First Avenue North
Minneapolis, MN 55401 USA

For reading levels and more information, look up this title at www.lernerbooks.com.

Main body text set in Metro Office 12/18. Typeface provided by Linotype AG.

Library of Congress Cataloging-in-Publication Data

Names: Markle, Sandra, author.
Title: The great rhino rescue : saving the southern white rhinos / by Sandra Markle.
Description: Minneapolis : Millbrook Press, [2018] | Audience: Age 9-12. | Audience: Grade 4 to 6. | Includes bibliographical references and index.
Identifiers: LCCN 2017040488 (print) | LCCN 2018002121 (ebook) | ISBN 9781541524729 (eb pdf) | ISBN 9781512444360 (lb : alk. paper)
Subjects: LCSH: White rhinoceros—Southern Africa—Conservation—Juvenile literature. | Animal rescue—South Africa—Juvenile literature.
Classification: LCC QL737.U63 (ebook) | LCC QL737.U63 M33 2018 (print) | DDC 599.66/80968—dc23

LC record available at https://lccn.loc.gov/2017040488

Manufactured in the United States of America
1-42510-26187-1/3/2018

TABLE OF CONTENTS

TROUBLE!

The fireball sun is low in the sky. Though night is coming, hot air still shimmers over the savanna in South Africa's Kruger National Park. A large female Southern white rhino plods through the lengthening shadows while her young calf trots beside her.

With a huff and a grunt, the mother rhino stops, and her calf stops too. She bends her big head to the ground and nips off a mouthful of grass to chew. The calf noses beneath the mother's belly by her hind legs and begins to nurse. For this calf, all is now right with the world. But the mother's ears twist to home in on an unusual sound in the rustling grass.

At first, a baby rhino has only bumps where its horns will grow. That way it doesn't hurt its mother while nursing.

No wild predators are a threat to her, but hunting lions or a pack of hyenas could hurt her baby. And even though the mother rhino doesn't see well enough to spy what's sneaking through the shadows, she has a keen sense of smell. When she sniffs a scent she knows means danger, she grunts. The pair bolts.

Rhinos can run as fast as 31 miles (50 km) an hour, but only for short bursts.

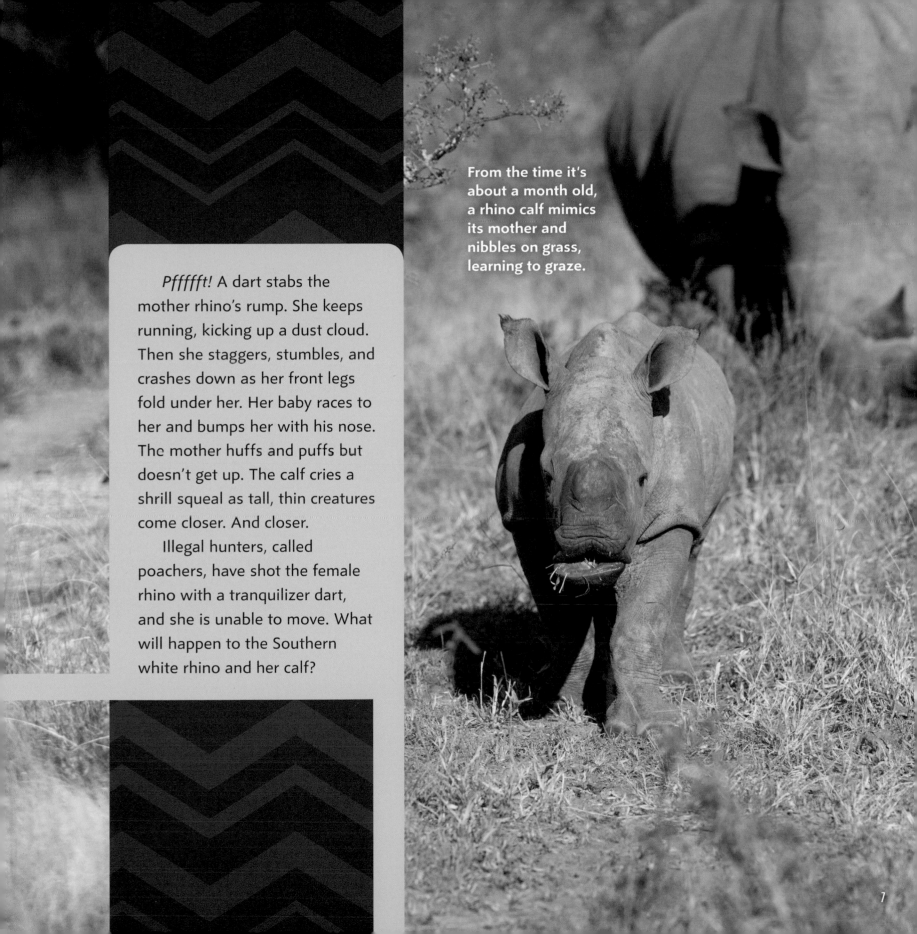

From the time it's about a month old, a rhino calf mimics its mother and nibbles on grass, learning to graze.

Pffffft! A dart stabs the mother rhino's rump. She keeps running, kicking up a dust cloud. Then she staggers, stumbles, and crashes down as her front legs fold under her. Her baby races to her and bumps her with his nose. The mother huffs and puffs but doesn't get up. The calf cries a shrill squeal as tall, thin creatures come closer. And closer.

Illegal hunters, called poachers, have shot the female rhino with a tranquilizer dart, and she is unable to move. What will happen to the Southern white rhino and her calf?

The Southern white rhino has two horns. The longer one in the front can grow to be almost 5 feet (1.5 m) long.

ONCE EXTINCT

The population of Southern white rhinos can't afford a single loss. Only about twenty thousand are left in the world, and with each passing year, the population shrinks. Southern white rhinos need rescuing—*again*.

Throughout most of the nineteenth century, people thought Southern white rhinos were extinct—that no more existed. Their numbers had begun to slip in the mid-seventeenth century after early European settlers arrived in southern Africa. The Europeans brought guns, and the big rhinos were an easy target. Some hunters killed rhinos for meat. Others hunted them just for sport. The settlers also cleared and farmed large areas of the savanna. This change in the rhino's habitat proved disastrous for the Southern white rhino population.

Why did losing sections of the savanna hurt the rhinos?

What Is a Savanna?

The African savanna is grassy, flat land with a scattering of low, shrubby trees. It is the perfect home for Southern white rhinos since adult rhinos are grass eaters and feed on about 120 pounds (54 kg) of grass every day. In fact, Southern white rhinos eat *only* grass! A rhino spends at least half of the time it is awake feeding. They get the water they need to survive from water holes and rivers. These water sources are important to rhinos for another reason, though. Rhinos wallow, or roll around, in the mud at the edges of water holes. Despite its armorlike skin that's almost a half-inch thick (1.27 cm), rhinos are sensitive to sunburn and insect bites. A mud coating protects their skin.

If water is available, a rhino will drink every day, but it can go up to five days without water.

Farming large areas of savanna limited the rhino's food supply. It also made finding a mate difficult. Southern white rhinos are territorial—they claim an area of land as their own and usually roam only in that area. A rhino will attack intruding rhinos to defend its territory. But it also avoids fights with other rhinos by marking its claim to the land. The rhino deposits piles of dung (solid wastes) as markers along the territory's borders. Sometimes, though, the scent message in these deposits isn't "Stay away!" A rhino's body chemistry packs other smells into its dung, such as whether the rhino is a male or a female and if it's seeking a mate. For rhinos to thrive, farmland needs to be spaced out to give them wildlife corridors through which they can connect with other rhinos of their own kind. Otherwise, the rhinos become isolated on their home territories and can't mate.

The Southern white rhino is one of the heaviest land animals. Males weigh as much as 5,511 pounds (2,500 kg)—about as much as a small forklift. So when two males fight for a mate, it's a *big* battle.

Male Southern white rhinos usually roam on their own and claim territories that may cover as little as 1 square mile (2.6 sq. km) or as much as 23 square miles (60 sq. km). They need larger areas where grass is scarce. Females roam much larger territories than males, and their territories usually overlap with those of several males—unless they are blocked by fenced farmland. Females may travel alone, or they may drift in and out of groups of other females and their calves.

A female Southern white rhino usually gives birth to one calf at a time.

Even where savanna areas remained, though, all the hunting meant few Southern white rhinos were left to mate and produce young. And an increasing human population turning even more savanna areas into farmland forced some of those few remaining rhinos to relocate. This relocation made it even harder for adult males and females to find each other, which was critical for the survival of the entire population.

In her lifetime, each female rhino only produces a few young to add to the population. Female Southern white rhinos don't begin to mate until they're six or seven years old. Males don't begin to mate until they are between ten and twelve years old. Once a female mates, she is pregnant for about sixteen months before giving birth. Then a mother rhino guards her calf for about eighteen months. A female can live to be about forty years old and, once she starts mating, she can add one offspring to the population roughly every two to three years. But predators may kill the calf. Or hunters may kill the mother, which can also lead to the calf's death.

With all of these factors working against the rhinos, they had very little chance of survival. But were all the Southern white rhinos *really* gone?

MIRACLE

In 1895 a group of fewer than one hundred Southern white rhinos was discovered—some accounts say fewer than fifty. That there were any at all was a miracle. So where were these remaining rhinos? And how did they manage to survive?

The surviving Southern white rhinos were discovered living in KwaZulu-Natal (now Hluhluwe–Imfolozi Park) in southeastern South Africa. This area had been set aside and reserved as a royal hunting ground for the king of the Zulu people. No one dared to go there without the king's permission. Hunters also stayed away because the region was infested with disease-carrying insects.

SOUTHERN WHITE RHINO RANGE

AFRICA

The increasing number of Southern white rhinos meant that, by the early 1960s, the population could be spread beyond South Africa into other countries.

KENYA

UGANDA

MOZAMBIQUE

ZAMBIA

NAMIBIA

ZIMBABWE

SOUTH AFRICA

SWAZILAND

BOTSWANA

Introduced to land

Reintroduced to land

Native land

Data retrieved from the IUCN Red List of Threatened Species

Once the small Southern white rhino herd was spotted, the local government wanted to protect the rhinos. So KwaZulu-Natal was set aside as a protected reserve, making the historical protection of this area official. This helped guarantee the survival of the rhinos, and the size of the Southern white rhino herd began to grow.

A crash is a group of rhinos. Because males often roam alone, only females and calves are usually in a crash.

The number of Southern white rhinos is recorded and tracked by the International Union for the Conservation of Nature (IUCN) Species Survival Commission African Rhino Specialist Group.

By the mid-twentieth century, the herd had grown so much that new young adult rhinos could no longer find grazing territories to claim within the protected KwaZulu-Natal. To continue increasing the Southern white rhino population, the government's conservation team captured small groups of males and females and relocated them. They were moved to other protected areas, such as Kruger National Park and private game ranches.

In 1960 a survey of the wild Southern white rhino population recorded 840 rhinos. Most were living in South Africa, with small numbers in nearby countries. Just eight years later, in 1968, another survey reported around 1,800 Southern white rhinos—more than double the previous count. The population of Southern white rhinos appeared to be heading toward a stable future.

But was it?

It's a Rhino's Life

The rhino weighs about 150 pounds (68 kg) at birth. No wonder a mother has only one baby at a time!

After birth, the mother immediately licks the newborn calf clean, and the young rhino is soon standing and walking. For its first weeks, the baby rhino may feed as often as every few hours, and it gains between 4.5 to 6.5 pounds (2 to 3 kg) each day. At just one month old, the rhino calf starts sampling grasses as well as nursing. By the time it is about eighteen months old, the baby rhino stops nursing and weighs nearly ten times more than at birth.

In addition to nursing and eating grass, a Southern white rhino calf eats some of its mother's dung. Why? It needs to gain the digestive bacteria essential for it to become a plant eater.

TOO VALUABLE

The Southern white rhino population seemed to be doing well and set to continue to grow. So South Africa and Namibia legalized hunting rhinos. But the governments of these countries limited the number that could be shot by auctioning off hunting rights to trophy hunters—hunters willing to pay to hunt rhinos for sport. Hunting Southern white rhinos was banned, however, in Zimbabwe, Kenya, and Uganda, where the reintroduced populations remained small.

In 1989 the price for a license to hunt a Southern white rhino soared to 92,000 South African rand—one rand was nearly equal to one US dollar at the time.

Rhino trophy hunting became even more strictly controlled in 1973, when the Convention on International Trade in Endangered Species (CITES) was founded to protect animals and plants. This organization regulated which rhinos could be hunted, limiting it mainly to old bulls past breeding age. These regulations allowed the population to continue growing. So by 2001 the Southern white rhino population had slightly more than doubled again to 11,670.

The future of the Southern white rhinos looked promising, but a change for the worse was on the horizon.

NOSING INTO TROUBLE

For centuries there had been a small market for rhino horns in the Middle East, where they were used to make handles for ceremonial daggers. There was also a market for rhino horns in Asia, especially Vietnam and China. In those countries, some people ground rhino horn into a powder, mixed it with water, and drank it as medicine. They believed powdered rhino horn lowered fevers, cured skin and bone diseases, and generally improved health.

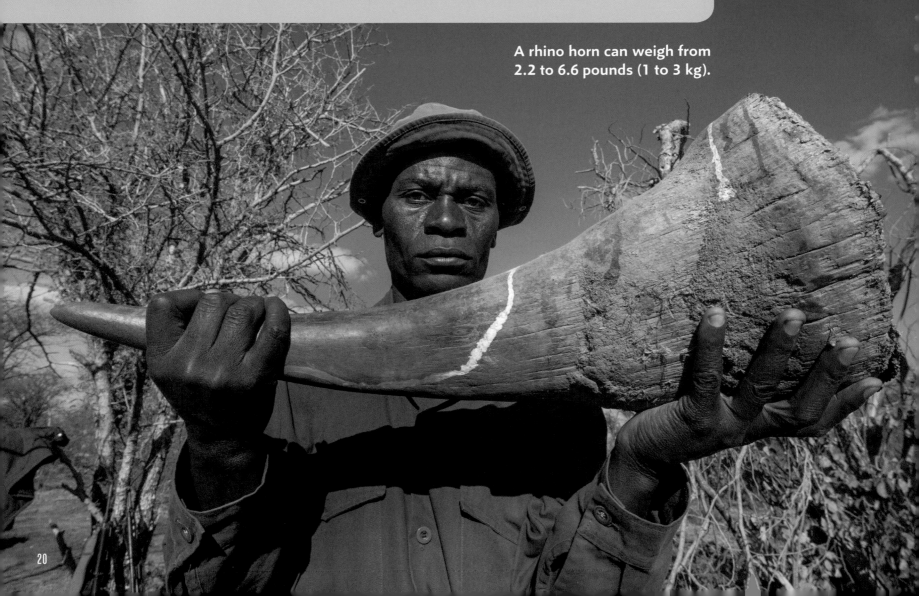

A rhino horn can weigh from 2.2 to 6.6 pounds (1 to 3 kg).

In the 1980s, as people became increasingly focused on protecting Earth's resources and the environment, a global concern for protecting all wildlife also developed. People became especially interested in protecting animals from poachers. Some countries made laws to halt the buying and selling of rhino horns. These laws helped stop poachers from targeting rhinos. In the 1990s, the Chinese government banned buying and selling rhino horn, which protected rhinos even more. Then, around 2008, a rumor that rhino horn could cure cancer began to spread throughout Asia. Immediately, the demand—and the price—for rhino horns soared, launching a huge increase in rhinos being attacked and often killed by poachers who only wanted their horns.

In 2007 the Save the Rhino International organization reported just 13 rhinos were poached. The South African government reported that 1,338 rhinos were killed by poachers in 2015.

ASIA

EUROPE

CHINA

ASSAM INDIA

TIBET

BHUTAN

MYANMAR (BURMA)

LAOS

NEPAL

VIETNAM

INDIA

Hong Kong

PACIFIC OCEAN

AFRICA

THAILAND

INDIAN OCEAN

MALAYSIA

KENYA

Singapore

TANZANIA

MALAWE

MOZAMBIQUE

ZAMBIA

Estimated number of horns illegally traded to Asia (2009–2015):
10,643 rhino horns*

Country or region supplying or transporting rhino horn

ZIMBABWE

Country with demand for rhino horn

SOUTH AFRICA

Trade route

*Based on data collected by the International Union for the Conservation of Nature (IUCN) from 2009–2012 and 2012–2015.

21

A rhino's horn can be carefully cut just like a fingernail and will grow back. However, rhino horn poachers risked being caught if they took the time to be that careful. So, instead, illegal hunters shot and killed rhinos and then quickly cut off their horns. Or worse, they darted the rhinos to tranquilize them and then hacked off their horns, leaving the animals with such serious facial wounds that they died.

With help from caring wildlife vets, some rhinos, like the one on the right, survived having their horns hacked off.

Not all the rhinos killed were Southern white rhinos. The other main kind of rhino living in Africa—black rhinos—were also attacked for their horns. But the Southern white rhinos were the hardest hit because there were more of them and, compared to black rhinos, they are usually very calm. Poachers could more easily sneak up close before the rhino ran away or charged to attack.

The result was Southern white rhinos were in danger of becoming extinct yet again—this time because of their valuable horns. Something had to be done to rescue them. But what?

The most reliable records of rhino poachings are kept in South Africa, which has the largest population of both wild black rhinos and white rhinos. These records show that increased security is helping to reduce poaching.

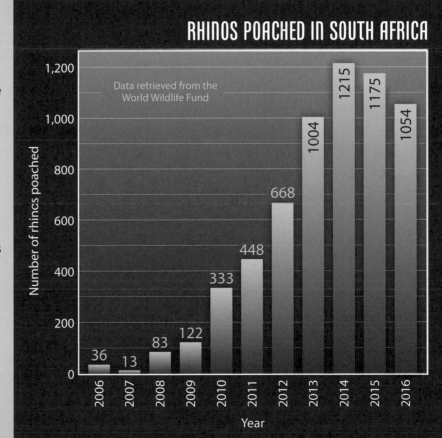

RHINOS POACHED IN SOUTH AFRICA

Data retrieved from the World Wildlife Fund

Number of rhinos poached

Year	
2006	36
2007	13
2008	83
2009	122
2010	333
2011	448
2012	668
2013	1004
2014	1215
2015	1175
2016	1054

MAKING THE HORNS WORTHLESS

One way to save rhinos from being attacked by poachers is to tranquilize them and carefully cut off their horns. But this still leaves a big flat horn about 3 inches (8 cm) high on the rhino's nose. That's enough to be valuable if it were completely removed. Additionally, the horn immediately starts to regrow, recovering about 1.6 pounds (0.7 kg) within a year and making the rhino attractive to poachers again.

A rhino's horn is so hard it has to be removed with a chain saw.

That's why Lorinda Hern, founder of the Rhino Rescue Project, worked with wildlife veterinarian Charles van Niekerk to come up with another way to protect rhinos—make the horns worthless.

Van Niekerk developed a special solution to inject into a rhino's horn. A pink dye was mixed with chemicals regularly given to rhinos to eliminate any internal parasites (living things that live in or on other living things at that host's expense). Because a rhino's horn is made up of lots of strawlike tubules, the solution spread throughout the horn. And it didn't hurt the rhino.

To inject this solution, Van Niekerk drilled several holes into a rhino's horn and then pumped in the chemical-dye solution.

25

What's Inside a Rhino's Horn?

A rhino's horn may look like part of the animal's skull, but it isn't. It's more like a patch on top of the skin supported by bony stalks on the skull and underneath the skin. The horn starts growing when a calf is about six months old. And it keeps growing about 4 inches (10 cm) longer each year for the rest of the rhino's life.

The structure of a rhino's horn is unique. In most animals with horns, such as cows, the horn is bone covered by a thin coating of keratin (the same fibrous protein that makes up human hair and nails). A rhino's horn, however, is completely made of keratin. Computer tomography (CT) scans reveal the rhino's horn is actually lots of keratin tubules embedded in more keratin. It's kind of like lots of hairs stuck together with hair gel. Calcium and melanin, two kinds of dense minerals, strengthen the center of the rhino's horn. These minerals keep the horn's core strong even as exposure to the weather and the sun's UV rays weakens the outer layers. That's why, when a rhino rubs its horn on the ground, rocks, or trees, the horn itself doesn't snap off. Instead, only the outer layers break off, which determines the horn's length and shape.

While researchers don't yet know how minerals are deposited in the core of a rhino's horn, like this one, they know it happens yearly in spurts. It may have to do with seasonal climate changes and having plenty of grass to eat.

Hern made sure there was lots of news coverage about rhino horns being injected. And said that drinking the dyed rhino horn powder could possibly make people feel ill. From the outside, the dyed horns looked just like any other horn, so poachers didn't touch the rhinos in any area where some had reportedly been treated with the chemical-dye solution.

But what could be done for the rhinos that survived an attack by poachers?

A little of the chemical-dye solution leaks out as the injector is removed.

HELPING THE SURVIVORS

Wildlife veterinarian Will Fowlds supports teams of veterinarians who help rhinos whose horns have been removed. One survivor, attacked in April 2015, was a female nicknamed Hope. In her case, Johan Joubert, Johan Marais, and Gerhard Steenkamp worked long and hard to save her. Fowlds said, "Hope's wounds were among the worst I'd ever seen."

The wounds were too deep and wide to close with a single operation. Instead, little by little—through a series of operations—the veterinarians eased the tissue and bone closer together. After each surgery, they wrapped Hope's wounds in bandages anchored in place with elastic bands like those used in human abdominal surgery. Then they covered the area with a shield. The team experimented with using different materials for this shield, including fiberglass, plastic, and even the hide from an elephant that had passed away at a local reserve. The goal was to create a shield that would fit the shape of Hope's face and withstand her natural urge to rub it against anything hard.

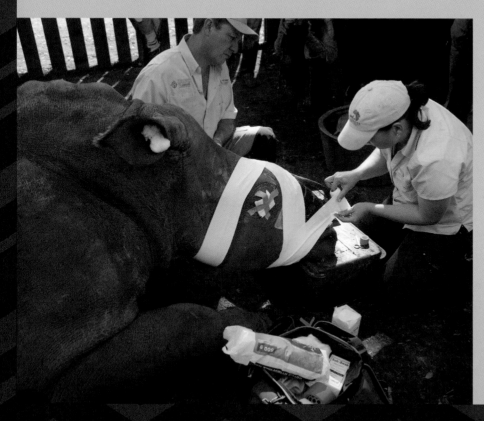

Poachers removed both of Hope's horns so deeply that her airways were open, making it hard for her to breathe.

Will Fowlds used skin grafts to help close the wounds on this rhino's face. A team from Saving the Survivors with the help of a dermatologist (a doctor who treats human skin disorders) performed earlier skin grafts.

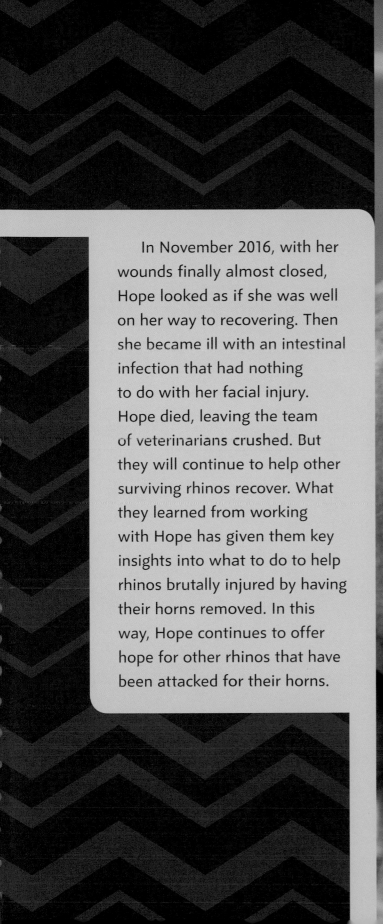

In November 2016, with her wounds finally almost closed, Hope looked as if she was well on her way to recovering. Then she became ill with an intestinal infection that had nothing to do with her facial injury. Hope died, leaving the team of veterinarians crushed. But they will continue to help other surviving rhinos recover. What they learned from working with Hope has given them key insights into what to do to help rhinos brutally injured by having their horns removed. In this way, Hope continues to offer hope for other rhinos that have been attacked for their horns.

Sometimes a rhino doesn't survive long enough to be helped. If the attacked rhino is a mother, her calf is orphaned. Lorinda Hern's Rhino Rescue Project in South Africa raises orphaned rhinos—both black rhinos and Southern white rhinos. Hern said, "It's not easy. Rhino calves wail and can actually die from depression, missing the bond they felt with their mothers."

A human helper comforts an orphaned rhino calf.

While young rhino calves live with a foster mother, human helpers feed them their bottles.

To help them survive, orphaned calves are penned up with a foster mother— any four-legged grazer, such as a cow, a sheep, or a goat. Older rhino calves of a similar age are penned together, and just as in the wild, they'll bond with one another and form a small herd.

When the young rhinos are old enough to graze and live on their own, they're released to well-protected areas, such as private game ranches. Hern said, "When you've hand reared a rhino calf for two or three years, you really care about it being watched over and staying safe."

PATROLLING AND RELOCATING

In Kruger National Park, people regularly patrol to keep an eye out for signs that rhino poachers have slipped into the park. These patrols face huge challenges because Kruger National Park covers 7,523 square miles (19,484 sq. km). And adult rhinos often roam alone over their territories. But once patrols spot any tracks or other signs of poachers in the park, special K9 units of dogs working with handlers try to find and arrest them. Henry Holsthyzen oversees this special K9 unit of handlers with strong, alert Belgian Malinois and other dog breeds typically used in police work.

Holsthyzen explained, "For this job, the first step is to train the dogs to ignore all the wild animals in the Park." So Holsthyzen's team uses scat (animal droppings) to get the dogs so used to the wild animal scents that they ignore them. Then the dogs are trained to track human scents.

The dogs are trained to tell the scent of their patrol team from that of strangers—the rhino poachers.

This man and his dog are members of the Kruger National Park anti-poaching K9 unit.

Once a report comes in from rangers that poachers may be in an area, the K9 anti-poaching teams rush into action. They usually go in by truck or, if it's a remote site, by helicopter.

While a few handlers control their dogs with whistle commands, most have them on long rope leads, which are like leashes. Holsthyzen explained, "My first concern is for the dog's safety. The bush can become a very tricky place—open savanna one minute, then very thick bush with snakes the next. And on a rope lead, handlers can manage their dogs quietly."

The dog alerts its handler by pulling or slackening up on the lead but not by barking. When the dogs find the poachers, their armed handlers arrest them. One of the most successful teams is a dog named Killer and his handler, Amos Mzimba. As of 2016, during four years of service, this pair has helped arrest seventy-seven poachers in Kruger National Park.

Besides having guards patrol for and stop poachers, an effort is under way in South Africa to protect wild rhinos by setting up Community Ownership Zones. The plan is for the government to partner with the people living near Kruger National Park and other places where rhinos roam wild. The goal is to make protecting the rhinos for tourism more profitable than poaching rhino horns.

Rhinos are relocated to protect them from poachers and, sometimes, to prevent inbreeding (mating of closely related animals that can pass on inherited diseases).

Most people in these areas welcome the project. The animals are valued as part of their cultural heritage. They want the rhinos to survive to live alongside future generations.

Sometimes, though, if there is a lot of poaching in an area, the only way to keep rhinos safe is to relocate them. Most often the rhinos are walked onto a truck and driven to their new home. However, in rugged areas, rhinos must be airlifted to safety.

Clearly, there are many different and creative ways that people are helping rhinos.

If a rhino needs to be relocated and the land is rugged, the rhino is tranquilized, suspended by its ankles below a helicopter, and flown to its new home.

Why Do Savannas Need Southern White Rhinos?

Southern white rhinos play a key role in shaping the area where they live. In fact, they've been called ecosystem engineers—they help their savanna home be exactly what it is.

Southern white rhinos eat a lot of grass and clip plants close to the ground. It's as if the rhinos regularly mow the grass wherever they roam. Without rhinos, the grasses would grow long, increasing the danger of far-ranging fires during dry seasons. The dung the rhinos deposit also helps fertilize the grasses and other plants so they grow better. And because rhinos regularly wallow at the edges of water holes, they help create areas other animals can use to get muddy, protecting themselves from the sun's burning rays.

A mud coat shields a rhino's skin from sunburn and insect bites.

GUARDING THE PRESENT

Whappa-whappa. *Whappa-whappa. Whappa-whappa.*

The helicopter sweeps so low its whirling blades raise a dust cloud. Through the haze, armed soldiers with dogs at their sides arrive by helicopter to catch the rhino poachers. But the trio of poachers hears the helicopter and flees.

Because the poachers knew the park was patrolled regularly, they'd used a tranquilizer gun to shoot the rhino. They didn't risk a noisy rifle shot that might have alerted a patrol but not have brought down the rhino. This time, even though the poachers sedated the mother, the soldiers arrive in the nick of time. The mother rhino's horns are uncut. She and her calf are safe.

A guard and his dog slide down a rope to the ground.

As soon as the tranquilizer begins to wear off, the mother rhino stirs and grunts to her calf. Meanwhile, the dogs lead the armed patrol to the poachers and the handlers arrest them. Then they wait with the prisoners for the other members of the patrol to arrive by truck.

Meanwhile, the mother rhino recovers enough to stand up. Unsteady at first, she wobbles on her big legs. Then she plods away with her calf beside her until she stops to rest. There, in the last light of the fading day, the mother grazes and her calf noses in to nurse.

The calf stays at its mother's side while she recovers.

For the moment, this Southern white rhino pair is safe.

Can the calf stay safe long enough to grow up and reproduce? Can the mother rhino stay safe long enough to mate again and add another calf to the Southern white rhino population?

Maybe Southern white rhinos will survive—thanks to people coming up with creative ways to make rhino horn unsellable. And thanks to people working tirelessly to guard rhinos, rehabilitate injured rhinos, and raise orphaned calves.

But the rhinos' future cannot be certain because another threat to rhinos surfaced in 2017. South Africa's Constitutional Court, its highest court, overturned the 2009 ban on trading rhino horn within the country. A number of landowners in South Africa have been raising and dehorning rhinos to protect them from attacks by poachers. But these rhino breeders have been stockpiling those valuable removed horns. Because of this group's political push, it's now legal to sell and buy rhino horn in South Africa. Even though exporting the horn to other countries remains illegal, the new law and the huge prices for rhino horns may lead to even more attacks on rhinos for their valuable horns.

There is still one sure way everyone can help rhinos survive—by spreading the truth. *Rhino horn does NOT cure cancer. Rhino horn does NOT help people in any way.* The only one who needs a rhino's horn is the rhino!

Southern white rhinos aren't white. The name white comes from the Afrikaans name for them—*weit*, which means "wide." It refers to their wide, square upper lip.

Helping Northern White Rhinos

The Northern white rhino population is at even greater risk than the Southern white rhino population. In fact, Northern white rhinos are currently listed as Critically Endangered—just one step from extinction. That's because, following the 2015 death of a female Northern white rhino at the San Diego Zoo, only three remain alive: one male and two females. But these three rhinos have never produced young and the male is so old there is little hope of him fathering a calf. A last-ditch effort is needed if Northern white rhinos are going to be saved from extinction.

The situation for Northern white rhinos is grim, but not hopeless. Scientists at the San Diego Zoo Institute for Conservation Research and the Leibniz Institute for Zoo and Wildlife Research in Berlin have a plan. Sperm and eggs (reproductive cells) collected from healthy young adults and frozen will be united to create embryos (unborn young). And scientists will implant those embryos in Southern white rhino females. The scientists believe Southern white rhinos are similar enough to Northern white rhinos to act as surrogate mothers for the developing young.

Will this plan work? It has not yet been tried, so it remains just a hope for preserving the future of Northern white rhinos.

The last Northern white rhinos are at the Ol Pejeta Conservancy in Kenya, Africa, and they're under constant guard.

Author's Note

Before I began researching this book, I'd known rhino horn poaching was a serious problem. However, my very first interview for this book made it clear to me that it was more than a threat to the rhino populations. It was simply—horribly—cruel. That realization also sent me in search of every hopeful angle—all the efforts being made to prevent rhinos from being attacked, injured, and killed for their horns. My focus was on the Southern white rhino because this kind of rhino has the largest population and is attacked most often. I was also fascinated that they had once been believed extinct and now are at risk again.

My very first interview for this book, with Dr. Lorinda Hern, brought home the personal aspect of this story. She told me about her childhood on a farm outside Johannesburg, South Africa. She described growing up with lots of wildlife around her but of her special attachment to the rhinos, which were extremely gentle animals. She shared the devastating experience of poachers attacking one female rhino, tranquilizing it, cutting open its airways to take the horns, and leaving it to die a slow death. That story made me value that she'd made it her life's work to find a safe way to make rhino horns worthless to poachers.

Then as my research continued, I talked to Dr. Richard Vigne at Ol Pejeta Conservancy and heard stories about raising rescued orphaned rhino calves and how they wailed for their lost mothers. They would sometimes even develop stomach ulcers from the stress of missing their mothers.

Even as I learned the hard sides of this story, I was inspired to continue searching for and sharing the hopeful sides of the story. I discovered the creative efforts to help adult survivors and orphaned calves and learned about all the time and effort spent helping, guarding, and even relocating rhinos to keep them safe.

Southern white rhinos are survivors. Through the efforts of hardworking, caring experts and volunteers, they're continuing to be valuable parts of their ecosystem. We have to help spread the word that rhinos are valuable—not for their horns—but as living ecosystem shapers.

Timeline

Note: Population numbers reported come from the International Union for the Conservation of Nature (IUCN) Species Survival Commission African Rhino Specialist Group.

1895 While Southern white rhinos were earlier believed to be extinct, a small group of fewer than 100 (some report as few as 50) is discovered in KwaZulu-Natal, South Africa.

1926 Kruger National Park opens in northeastern South Africa.

1929 The IUCN reports the number of Southern white rhinos to be at 150.

1960 The IUCN reports the number of Southern white rhinos to be at 840.

1968 The IUCN reports the number of Southern white rhinos to be at 1,800. The first legal hunt is held in South Africa.

1973 The Convention on International Trade in Endangered Species (CITES) is founded and increases control of rhino trophy hunting.

1980 Many countries make it illegal to buy and sell rhino horn, beginning a decade of slowed demand for rhino horn.

1984 The IUCN reports the number of Southern white rhinos to be at 3,800.

1989 The amount trophy hunters are willing to pay for a rhino peaks at 92,000 rand (one South African rand and one US dollar were nearly equal at that time).

1988 Sweetwaters Game Reserve is founded on the Ol Pejeta Ranch in Kenya, Africa, to protect black rhinos and other wildlife. Over time, it expands and becomes Ol Pejeta Conservancy.

1990 People practicing traditional Chinese medicine stop prescribing rhino horn, beginning a decade of even less demand for it.

1991 The South African government passes the Theft of Game Act, allowing landowners to claim rhinos identified with a brand or ear tag even if they leave their property and to be compensated for any killed by poachers.

1995 The IUCN reports the number of Southern white rhinos to be at 7,563.

2001–2007 The IUCN reports the number of Southern white rhinos rising from 11,670 to 17,474.

2008 Rumors begin spreading that drinking powdered rhino horn can cure cancer.

2010 The IUCN reports the number of Southern white rhinos to be at 20,170.

2013 The IUCN reports the number of Southern white rhinos to be at 20,405. This is a much smaller increase than previously recorded.

2017 South Africa's Constitutional Court overturns a ban on trading rhino horn within the country, but the ban on international trade remains.

What is one thing you would like to be able to add to this timeline in the future?

Source Notes

28 William Fowlds, telephone interview with author, March 23, 2017.

30 Lorinda Hern, telephone interview with author, April 20, 2016.

31 Ibid.

32 Henry Holsthyzen, telephone interview with author, May 11, 2016.

33 Ibid.

Glossary

calf: baby rhinoceros

dehorning: cutting off a rhino's horn

dung: an animal's solid waste droppings

ecosystem: a community of animals that interact within a natural environment

extinct: wiped out, no longer having any living members

habitat: natural home environment of a plant or animal

parasite: a living thing that lives in or on another living thing at that host's expense

poachers: hunters who try to capture or kill animals illegally

predator: an animal that hunts and eats other living things in order to live

prey: an animal that is hunted and eaten for food by another animal

savanna: a grassy plain with a few scattered trees

species: one kind of living thing

territory: an area over which an animal normally travels in search of food or a mate

tranquilize: to use a drug to put an animal to sleep temporarily. The drug is often given by a syringe or dart.

Find Out More

Check out these books and websites to discover even more:

Carson, Mary Kay. *Emi and the Rhino Scientist.* Boston: Houghton Mifflin Harcourt Books for Young Readers, 2007.
Share the real-life work of scientist Terri Roth with one Sumatran rhinoceros in the Sumatran jungle.

Kessler, Cristina. *Our Secret, Siri Aang.* New York: Philomel Books, 2004.
This fictional story is told from the perspective of Namelok, a Maasai girl in modern Kenya, who witnesses the birth of a black rhino and vows to protect it from poachers.

Newman, Patricia. *Zoo Scientists to the Rescue.* Minneapolis: Millbrook Press, 2017.
Explore how zoo scientists are studying black rhinos to learn how to better protect them in their natural habitat.

Pope, Kristen. *Black Rhinos.* Avon, MA: Child's World, 2015.
Take a closer look at this species of endangered rhino. Compare how it is similar to white rhinos and how it is different.

San Diego Zoo—Southern White Rhino Calf Explores New Habitat
https://www.youtube.com/watch?v=Tb2m_ZwkVcQ
Don't think rhinos are cute? Check out this newborn in action.

Save the Rhino For Kids
https://www.savetherhino.org/rhino_info/for_kids
This site includes lots of facts as well as a sewing pattern for making a tiny rhino of your very own.

You Would Never Guess This Is What a Rhino Sounds Like
https://www.youtube.com/watch?v=LNCC6ZYI3SI
Check out this video to hear the many noises baby white rhinos make.

Index

Photo Acknowledgments

The images in this book are used with the permission of: © Tony Heald/Minden Pictures, p. 1; © Richard Du Toit/Minden Pictures, p. 4; © Roland Seitre/Minden Pictures, p. 5; Rebecca Yale/Moment/Getty Images, p. 6; Heinrich van den Berg/Stockbyte/Getty Images, p. 7; © Joel Sartore/National Geographic Creative, pp. 8–9; Denny Allen/Gallo Images/Getty Images, p. 10; © Michael Hutchinson/Minden Pictures, p. 11; © Gerry Ellis/Minden Pictures, pp. 12–13; © Hiroya Minakuchi/Minden Pictures, pp. 14–15; © Laura Westlund/Independent Picture Service, pp. 14, 21, 23; © ROBIN MOORE/National Geographic Stock, p. 16; Danita Delimont/Gallo Images/Getty Images, p. 17; Lanz von Horsten/Gallo Images/Getty Images, pp. 18–19; © Pete Oxford/Minden Pictures, p. 20; Brent Stirton/Reportage Archive/Getty Images, pp. 22–23; Michel Gunther/Biosphoto/Getty Images, p. 24; © Rhino Rescue Project, pp. 25, 26, 27; AP Photo/Denis Farrell, pp. 28, 38; © Neil Aldridge/naturepl.com, p. 29; Gallo Images/Getty Images, p. 30; Martin Harvey/Corbis Documentary/Getty Images, pp. 30–31; STEFAN HEUNIS/AFP/Getty Images, pp. 32, 33; Gerald Hinde/Gallo Images/Getty Images, p. 34; AP Photo/Gallo Images/Rex Features, p. 35; Patrice Correia/Biosphoto/Getty Images, pp. 36–37; Gail Shotlander/Moment/Getty Images, p. 39; Martin Harvey/Corbis Documentary/Getty Images, pp. 40–41; AP Photo/Sakchai Lalit, p. 41; James Balog/The Image Bank/Getty Images, p. 42; AP Photo/Ann & Steve Toon/Solent News/FEREX, p. 43.

Cover and design elements: alexokokok/Shutterstock.com (grass); © Ignacio Yufera/FLPA/Minden Pictures (rhino); Alexandra Giese/Shutterstock.com (back cover).